Growing up in
SIKHISM

Andrew Clutterbuck

Series editor: Jean Holm

What is this book about?

One of the most interesting ways to learn about a religion is to try to see it through the eyes of children who are growing up in a religious family. In this way we can discover something of what it *feels* like to belong to the religion.

In the books in this series we shall be finding out how children gradually come to understand the real meaning of the festivals they celebrate, the scriptures and other stories they hear, the ceremonies they take part in, the symbols of their religion and the customs and traditions of their religious community. This should provide a good foundation for going on to a wider study of the religions.

The five books in this series deal with the main religions that are found in Britain today: Christianity, Hinduism, Islam, Judaism and Sikhism. However, some things are more important in one religion than in another. For example, festivals play a bigger part in the lives of Jewish children than they do in the lives of Sikh children, and the scriptures play a bigger part in the lives of Muslim children than they do in the lives of Hindu children, so although many of the same topics are dealt with in all the books, the pattern of each book is slightly different.

There are differences within every religion as well as between religions, and even a very long book could not describe the customs and beliefs of all the groups that make up a religion. In these books we may be learning more about one of the groups, or traditions, within the religion, but there will be references to the different ways in which other groups practise their faith.

In this series of books we are using BCE (Before the Christian Era) and CE (in the Christian Era) instead of BC and AD, which refer to Christian beliefs about the significance of Jesus.

How to use this book

Some of you will be studying religions for the first time. Others may already have learnt something about places of worship or festivals, and you will be able to gain greater understanding and fit what you know into a wider picture of the religion.

As you learn about how children grow up in a religion, prepare a display, or perhaps make a large class book. You will find some suggestions of activities in the text, but you will be able to think of many more. If your display is good enough it might be possible to put it up in the hall or in a corridor so that lots of people can see it. Try to show what it feels like to be on the 'inside' of the religion, so that other pupils and teachers and visitors to the school will be able to learn about the religion from the point of view of the children who are growing up in it.

Contents

The words in the glossary are printed in **bold** type the first time they appear in the book.

੧ੴ Living

The langar

*"The best times were the meals in the **gurdwara**. We all ate together in a large dining room and that made it really special. We were like one big family with everyone joining in to help. There was always a lot of work to do in the gurdwara. Often a group of us helped with the **langar**, that's what we call the meal. We rushed around making sure everything was clean and everyone had enough to eat. My favourite job was handing out table napkins because that meant I could talk to everybody. It gave me a nice feeling being so busy and watching other people enjoying their food. My dad told me it was because I was doing something for nothing."*

Like all children, Sikh children learn best by joining in. They do what their parents and other adults do. In the gurdwara, children and adults prepare and serve food given by members of the community. Every gurdwara has a shared kitchen – a langar – and a dining room so that everyone can have a meal together at the end of the service. To eat together is one way of showing that all people are equal.

The traditional custom of sharing food with everyone goes back a long way. It all started with the ten Sikh teachers or **Gurus** who lived between 1469 and 1708 (→ page 25). Each of these Gurus had a langar where everyone ate together. They thought it taught people a very important lesson. At that time, Hindus believed that every family belonged to a larger group called a **caste**, and that different castes should avoid eating together. There is a very popular story about Guru Amar Das and the Muslim Emperor, Akbar, ruler of India.

Emperor Akbar travelled many miles to see Guru Amar Das and his Sikh community at Goindwal. When he arrived, he asked to see the Guru straight away. He was told that this could not be arranged until he had eaten a meal in the langar. Akbar went to the langar and sat and ate and talked with the other people there. Many of the people were amazed to see the Emperor of India sharing food with them. Akbar thought the simple food was so delicious he could eat more and more of it. When the Guru appeared the Emperor bowed down to touch the Guru's feet. Emperor Akbar was so happy he offered the

Guru a large plot of land to pay for the important lesson he had learned. Akbar said he realised now that everyone is equal and that everyone deserves kindness and generosity. The Guru could not accept the land because langar is provided free as a gift from God and the community. So, Emperor Akbar gave it to the Guru's daughter to be used for widows and orphans.

Helping in the gurdwara

When meals are served in the gurdwara Sikh children help by cooking or serving food. First, they might clean the tables and set out all the stainless steel utensils, serve the food and then make sure everyone has enough water to drink with their meal. Finally, they might help with the cleaning and washing up. This can mean quite a lot of work.

Everybody is made welcome when they visit a gurdwara. They will be given something to eat and drink to make sure they feel part of the community.

"When my baby brother was born my family provided all the food for the langar. I helped with the shopping and that meant buying large sacks of flour, potatoes and other vegetables. The night before, lots of our friends came to help us prepare all the food. It took hours and we didn't get to bed until late. In the morning there was still a lot of cooking to do. It was no easy job cooking food for three hundred people. I think it was worth it though because everyone enjoyed the meal and I felt really pleased to have helped at every stage."

Inside the gurdwara there is a rota where people place their names if they want to provide the food or help with the cooking and serving. Providing food for the langar is so popular it is sometimes difficult to find a space on the rota.

Buying, cooking and serving food for a whole congregation is an enormous task. Look at the menu for ten people below. Just think how much food you would need for three hundred people!

Channa

2 lb (900 g) Chickpeas
2 lb (900 g) Potatoes
1 lb (450 g) Onions
4 Cloves garlic

Dhal

1 lb 4 oz (560 g) Whole green lentils
2 lb (900 g) Onions
2 lb (900 g) Butter
4–6 Fresh chillies
4 Cloves garlic
Fresh ginger
Garam masala and turmeric

Yoghurt

15 fl oz (0.43 litres)
Natural yoghurt

Chapattis

4–6 lbs (1.8–2.7 kg) Wholemeal flour
Water

Rice pudding

2 lb (900 g) Rice
2 lb (900 g) Sugar
6 Pints milk
Sultanas/Chopped almonds

Fresh Fruit

Apples
Oranges
Bananas

---

1 Using the information opposite, find out how much food you would need to provide a langar for either your school or your year. You could make a display showing the quantities needed.
2 See if you can find any Indian recipes which would include the ingredients used in the langar.

Notice that there are no meat or eggs in any of the dishes served in the langar. Many Sikhs are vegetarians and this makes sure that everyone can join in the meal. Everyone helps at some stage – whether they are men or women, whether they are factory workers, bank managers, teachers or shop assistants – and everyone will eat together. Although men and women might eat at separate tables, this is a traditional custom and does not mean that one is more important than the other.

Seva – selfless work

"We don't wear shoes inside the gurdwara; they're all left in the entrance hall. Once, my friends and I cleaned all the shoes that were there. When people left, it was funny watching them trying to find their own shoes!

We don't just do things at the gurdwara. At home we all help with the jobs that need doing. My mum has taught me how to cook. My favourite is Semolina Halva. It's light and fluffy and we eat it after meals. My brother doesn't like cooking, but he likes eating."

Sikh children learn that providing langar and helping others is called **seva**. This means selfless work for the benefit of other people. They also learn that seva can be done anywhere and for anyone.

Can you think of any other types of seva that children might see their parents performing in their local community? Try to make a list first and then look at page 60.

Seva is the first step towards understanding that everyone is equal. Nobody is more important than anyone else. Sikh children also learn that this belief must be put into practice. At the same time seva helps Sikh children to learn how to look after themselves.

Here is your chance to try some Indian cooking. Semolina Halva is very easy to make.

Semolina Halva (for five people)

475 ml Water	250 g Fine-grained semolina
140 g Sugar	20 g Blanched and chopped almonds
4 tsp Vegetable oil	25 g Sultanas
¾ tsp Finely crushed cardamom seeds	

1 Boil the water and sugar in a saucepan then put it to one side.
2 Heat the butter gently until it melts. Then gently fry the semolina until it is golden brown.
3 Stir in the almonds, sultanas and cardamom seeds.
4 Very slowly, pour in the sugared water and cook gently for another five minutes.

Your halva can be served hot or at room temperature.

If this recipe is made without the sultanas, almonds and cardamom seeds it is like **karah prashad**. A small amount of this is given to everybody at the end of the service in the worship room. To be used in a gurdwara, karah prashad must be prepared in a special way (⟶ page 23).

Going to the gurdwara

"The gurdwara is like another home. Lots of my friends go there and it's always warm and comfortable. In the entrance hall we take off our shoes. This makes it even more like home and means that everyone moves about very quietly. We also have to make sure our heads are covered. Then we go into the main room where our holy book, the **Guru Granth Sahib***, is placed."*

The word 'gurdwara' means 'house of the Guru'. A guru is a teacher who leads people from darkness and ignorance to light and understanding. The most important object in the gurdwara is the Guru Granth Sahib. It is treated as a living teacher. This is why it is very important to learn to behave properly in the worship room. Sikh children learn to call it Shri Guru Granth **Sahib** Ji, which is giving it a title of great respect.

The layout of a typical worship room. Notice the position of the Guru Granth Sahib.

"My dad used to give me some money. When I went into the worship room I walked straight up to the front and placed the money in a slot in a large box. Then I knelt and bowed right down to the ground in front of the Guru Granth Sahib with my forehead touching the floor. Without turning round I then walked backwards to find a place to sit. When we sat down we had to be careful that our feet didn't point towards the Guru Granth Sahib. This would be very disrespectful. Anyway, it's more comfortable to sit cross-legged."

Men and women sit separately in the worship room so children sit either on their father's or their mother's side. When they are very young they can choose whom they wish to sit with.

1   Start your own Punjabi word list. Write the meaning of the word beside it and try to use it in a sentence of your own.

2   Make a list of the ways in which the Guru Granth Sahib is shown respect and honour. You may like to illustrate these in a series of pictures. You can add more to your list as you learn more about the Guru Granth Sahib.

The Guru Granth Sahib

Children start going to the gurdwara from when they are very young. At first they don't understand everything that happens. Gradually they will see that the centre of all the attention is the Guru Granth Sahib. The Guru Granth Sahib is placed at the front of the worship room on a **takht**. As children, Sikhs hear the story of how the last of the ten Gurus, Guru Gobind Singh, gave his followers a very important message. He said that after his death there would be no more human gurus. In their place a book called the **Adi Granth** was to be the only teacher of the community. From that time on it was known as the Guru Granth Sahib.

The throne

Here is a description of how the Guru Granth Sahib is seated in the gurdwara.

> A small wooden base, the **manji sahib**, is placed on a raised platform. The manji sahib is covered with a cloth.
>
> Three small cushions are placed on top of the cloth. These support the Guru Granth Sahib and make sure that it is tilted slightly for easy reading.
>
> Richly decorated cloths are spread over the manji sahib.
>
> The Guru Granth Sahib is placed on top of these cloths.
>
> The Guru Granth Sahib is covered with a cloth called a **rumala** when it is not being read.
>
> A canopy or cover is placed over the Guru Granth Sahib. This is called a **chanani**.
>
> A **chauri** is waved over the Guru Granth Sahib. This is like the fly-whisk which in olden times was waved to show respect to very important people in India.

By behaving in the proper way children learn that the Guru Granth Sahib is to be respected as the voice of the True Guru, God. As a teacher, the Guru Granth Sahib must be treated with honour. In the morning the Guru Granth Sahib is brought from the room where it has been allowed to rest for the night. It is placed on a cloth and carried on the head of a Sikh in a procession to the worship room.

Draw sketches to show how the Guru Granth Sahib is seated in the worship room. Perhaps you could make a model of the takht using cardboard boxes and brightly coloured cloths.

The Guru Granth Sahib is a collection of 5,894 religious songs praising God. These songs or **shabads** were written by several of the first ten Gurus and by a number of other Sikhs. There are also shabads written by Muslims and Hindus included in the Guru Granth Sahib. This shows that everyone can receive special words from God, not just Sikhs.

Every copy of the Guru Granth Sahib has exactly the same number of pages – 1,430. Each of the shabads will appear on the same page in each copy.

The Guru Granth Sahib is not worshipped as God, but it is respected and honoured as a living teacher. It is the guide to life and to closeness with the True Guru, God. The teachings of the Guru Granth Sahib are called **gurbani**. They are the 'Words of the Guru'.

The Guru Granth Sahib always occupies a position of honour. All important ceremonies, such as naming, taking **amrit**, and marriage, must take place in its presence (⟶ pages 47, 57, 53). The only exception is a funeral.

A woman granthi reading from the Guru Granth Sahib. Notice the chauri at the front of the picture.

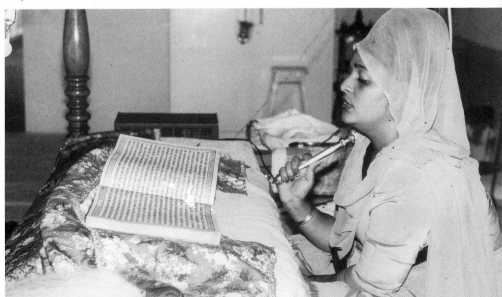

Understanding Punjabi

At the gurdwara Sikh children hear people reading from the Guru Granth Sahib. The reader, or **granthi**, can be any man or woman who is able to read the Guru Granth Sahib.

"I speak Punjabi at home but I can't understand everything that happens at the gurdwara, because the Guru Granth Sahib is written like poetry and some of the words and expressions are unusual. That makes parts of it difficult to understand."

Most Sikh children have no problems understanding any announcements or talks in the gurdwara. This is because they are given either in modern Punjabi or, occasionally, in English. But the Guru Granth Sahib is written in an older form of Punjabi and some shabads are in other Indian languages. The Guru Granth Sahib is always read in its original language so it is very important to learn to understand this older form of Punjabi and the other languages where necessary.

For children who grow up in the State of Punjab in India there are very few problems with reading or understanding the meaning of the Guru Granth Sahib. They speak Punjabi at home and at school. Most of them learn how to read and write in Punjabi at school. They read books and poetry written in Punjabi and many of them also speak and study other Indian languages. By the age of ten or eleven they are able to read the Guru Granth Sahib. Children in other countries can usually speak some Punjabi, which they have learned from their parents. But it is only at home and with Punjabi-speaking friends that they will talk in the language. Also, many of them may not be able to read and write in Punjabi. Gradually, more schools in Britain are providing lessons for Sikh children to learn Punjabi.

Punjabi lessons

*"I started Punjabi lessons at the gurdwara when I was seven. Some children start at five. At first I was worried that I wouldn't be able to keep up but we had a good **giani** and learning the alphabet was very easy. It was only later that it got more difficult. When I started secondary school I stopped going. My dad said I could start learning again when I felt ready."*

The gurdwara usually organises Punjabi language classes either after school or for a few hours at the weekend. The lessons are held in separate rooms at the gurdwara. It can take a long time to be able to read the Guru Granth Sahib because it has a very complicated style. Many children who attend these classes will be able to read from the Guru Granth Sahib by the time they are adults.

A giani is a man or woman who is an expert in Punjabi and has spent many years studying the Guru Granth Sahib.

Gurmukhi

Whenever Punjabi is written down it is always written in the **Gurmukhi** script. So Sikh children speak Punjabi and read and write in Gurmukhi.

Many of the first Sikhs did not need to know how to read or write. They were farmers, blacksmiths and weavers. Those who could read and write used an old alphabet which couldn't represent all the Punjabi words and sounds. The second Guru, Guru Angad Dev, knew that it was important for the teachings of Guru Nanak to be written down accurately. Guru Angad Dev worked hard to produce a script which would be easy to read and to learn. He called this writing Gurmukhi which means 'the language of the Guru'. Guru Angad Dev started schools to teach everyone the Gurmukhi script.

Sikh children need to learn to read and write in Gurmukhi. See if you can identify the Gurmukhi letters on the blackboard (→ p. 14).

Learning the Gurmukhi script

First, children learn the Gurmukhi alphabet. This is written from left to right like English. While English characters 'sit' on a line, Gurmukhi characters 'hang' from a line. And unlike English there are no capital letters in Gurmukhi.

GURMUKHI CHARACTERS

Would you like to try your hand at some Gurmukhi? This chart shows that there are thirty-five characters in the Gurmukhi alphabet. The letters are in the same order in which they would be in a Punjabi dictionary.

Underneath each Gurmukhi character is the English letter which shows us how to pronounce it. This is called 'transliterating'. Transliteration changes the Gurmukhi script into the Roman script which English-speaking people can read.

You will notice that some of the transliterations end in an 'h'. This helps you to tell the difference between the Gurmukhi characters. It will also help you with the pronunciation. The transliteration for this character ਥ is 'th'. This means that after the 't' there is a short 'h' sound, as in the word 'pot-hole'. This is the same for every letter with an 'h' in the transliteration except 'ch' which is pronounced as it is in the English word 'child'.

The first three characters are vowels. As well as these vowel characters there are nine other vowel signs (see the chart at the top of page 15). Some English words have been given in this chart to help with your pronunciation. And there is a transliteration for each of the letters.

GURMUKHI VOWEL SIGNS									
Sign	ਾ	ਿ	ੀ	ੁ	ੂ	ੇ	ੈ	ੋ	ੌ
Position	ਕਾਰ	ਪਿਲ	ਪੀਲ	ਪੁਲ	ਪੂਲ	ਬੇਟ	ਬੈਟ	ਸੋਕ	ਸੌਕ
Pronunciation	car	pill	peel	pull	pool	bet	bait	soak	sock
Transliteration	a	i	ī	u	ū	e	ai	ō	o

Notice how the vowel signs are put either between characters, above or beneath them. The only exception is the second sign which is put before the character that it is sounded after.

There are two Gurmukhi letters and two vowel signs in this word:
ਗੁਰੂ
Read from left to right and transliterate the word into Roman script. Remember to transliterate the first character, then the vowel that is underneath it, then the second character and then the vowel that is underneath that.

This word has four characters and three vowel signs: ਗੁਰਮੁਖੀ

You can check your answer with the title of this chapter.

Here is the name of the first Guru: ਨਾਨਕ   At the end of this word there are two Gurmukhi characters together without a vowel sign separating them. When letters appear like this there is sometimes an 'a' placed between them when transliterating.

After the names of the first, second and fifth Gurus this word appears: ਦੇਵ   . It means 'the holy'.

The name of the second Guru introduces another rule. Two characters are sometimes joined at the top by a mark like this ੰ This is transliterated as an 'n'. ਅੰਗਦ

The third and fourth Gurus have second names which mean 'servant' or 'follower': ਅਮਰ ਦਾਸ   ਰਾਮ ਦਾਸ

The fifth Guru: ਅਰਜਨ ਦੇਵ

The names of the sixth and seventh Gurus include the second vowel sign: ਹਰਗੋਬਿੰਦ   ਹਰਰਾਇ

Remember that this must go after the character.

The name of the eighth Guru has two new signs. A dot underneath this character ਸ should be transliterated as 'sh'. It is pronounced halfway between 's' and 'sh'. A small ੍ sign underneath a letter is transliterated as an 'r'. ਹਰਿਕ੍ਰਿਸ਼ਨ

These last two names should now be easy: ਤੇਗ ਬਹਾਦਰ   ਗੋਬਿੰਦ ਸਿੰਘ

Check how well you did with the list of the ten Gurus on page 25.

Finally, here is one of the greetings Sikhs would use when meeting each other. Out of respect, Sikh children would place a ਜੀ afterwards if they were talking to older people:

ਸਤ ਸ੍ਰੀ ਅਕਾਲ   The greeting means 'Truth is eternal' (⟶ page 18). To reply, you would use the same words.

Music for worship

"As well as learning Punjabi, we also learned how to sing the shabads from the Guru Granth Sahib. The service at the gurdwara has a lot of singing. I only join in sometimes, but I can follow the rhythm of the music quite well."

*"One evening a week I went to learn to play the **jori** and the **baja**. We had a teacher who travelled every week from London to our gurdwara. He was one of the best teachers I've ever had. He was blind but his hearing was excellent and he could tell exactly what mistakes we made."*

Music and singing are important in Sikh worship. As well as the baja and jori, two other instruments are shown.

The two instruments most commonly used in the gurdwara are the baja and the jori. The baja, or harmonium, is played by pumping air through a chamber with one hand. The other hand is used to play the keyboard. The jori are two drums, each with a piece of goatskin stretched across one end only. The narrower drum is played using just the fingertips. For the broader one the player uses either the fingertips, the base of the palm or the whole open hand. There are usually three musicians in the service. Two of them play the baja and the third plays the jori. All three lead the singing in the gurdwara. The singing of shabads is called **kirtan**.

Both boys and girls learn shabads from the Guru Granth Sahib. But it is more often boys who learn to play the instruments. However, more girls are learning now as well. Some children are lucky and have their own instruments at home where they can practise.

It's hard work learning any musical instrument. Sikh children learn without printed words or music. By following the teacher's example and instructions, they learn by heart the words and music they need for the gurdwara. Children who have mastered the baja or jori sometimes play during the service.

All the Gurus encouraged music and singing. They thought it helped people both to understand themselves and to come closer to the True Guru, God. Here is one of the stories Sikh children hear which tells how powerful music and singing can be.

On one of their many travels together Guru Nanak and his friend, the Muslim musician **Bhai** Mardana, met a man called Sajjan. True to his name, which meant 'good friend', he would welcome everyone travelling through the area to stay with him and rest for the night. However, while they were sleeping he would kill his victims and take their money and clothes. Thinking Guru Nanak was a wealthy man, Sajjan invited him to stay for the night. After they had eaten and talked together for a long time, Sajjan became restless. He urged the Guru to go to bed. Instead, Guru Nanak asked Mardana to play a tune. Guru Nanak's shabad filled the room. Sajjan listened and soon realised that the song was for him. The words pierced his heart, he saw all the evil he had done and he began to cry. He fell down at the Guru's feet and asked for forgiveness. Guru Nanak told him to give away everything he had and live in peace with the True Guru, God.

> Try listening to songs and different types of music. Record how they make you feel. Can you explain how they helped you to feel this way?

Learning prayers

*"I must have learned some of the prayers when I was very young. The first of the longer prayers from the Guru Granth Sahib I learned from my mum. This was the **Mool Mantra**. When my grandad came to see us Mum made me say it for him. By the time I was nine I could say the whole of the **Anand Sahib**. I learned that at the gurdwara. Everyone says this near the end of the service. It made a lot of difference being able to join in. I felt like a true Sikh."*

You have already seen one of the first prayers Sikh children learn. This is the greeting on page 16. 'Sat shri akal' is used by parents to welcome friends to their home and when they meet Sikhs elsewhere. It says that they believe that 'Truth is eternal'.

Here is another prayer which children often hear in the home and at the gurdwara: ਵਾਹਿ ਗੁਰੂ

This means 'Wonderful Lord' (**Vahiguru**). It is often repeated on its own to help thinking and meditating on God. In the gurdwara service on page 23 you can see this prayer and a slightly longer version. Sometimes this version is used as a greeting. One person says the first part of the sentence and the second part is said as the reply.

Here is the Mool Mantra. It is a very short prayer but a very important one. It sums up everything Sikhs believe about God. It is the first passage in the Guru Granth Sahib and is usually the first prayer that Sikh children learn.

There is one God,
Truth is God's Name,
The Creator, indwelling,
Without fear, without hate,
Timeless and without form;
Beyond death – the Enlightened One:
Known by the Guru's grace.

Prayer books

"At home we have some prayer books which we use in the morning and evening to say our prayers. Some of these we keep out on the bookshelves and others we wrap carefully in clean cloths. This keeps the dust off them."

Most families have small prayer books at home. A daily prayer book, or **nit-nem**, contains shabads which are used in daily prayers. Many of these shabads are from the Guru Granth Sahib. Other songs come from a separate book called the **Dasam Granth**. This contains all the shabads of Guru Gobind Singh. Sometimes the Guru Granth Sahib is called the Adi Granth. This shows that it is more important than any other book, including the Dasam Granth. Many families also have a longer form of prayer book – a **gutka**. This contains the complete nit-nem together with other songs and prayers for special occasions.

Ik Onkār

ਸਤਿਨਾਮੁ

Sat(i) nām(u)

ਕਰਤਾ ਪੁਰਖੁ

Kartā-purakh(u)

ਨਿਰਭਉ   ਨਿਰਵੈਰੁ

Nirbhau   Nirvair(u)

ਅਕਾਲ ਮੂਰਤਿ

Akāl-mūrat(i)

ਅਜੂਨੀ   ਸੈਭੰ

Ajūnī   Saibha'ng

ਗੁਰਪ੍ਰਸਾਦਿ

Gurparsād(i)

This is the text of the Mool Mantra from a nit-nem. Beneath each line there is a transliteration. A nit-nem sometimes includes transliterations to help children and adults who can't read Gurmukhi to pray in Punjabi.

1 Copy out the words of the Mool Mantra in English and in the Gurmukhi script.
2 Try learning the Mool Mantra by heart. Say it in Punjabi to get a feeling of the poetry of the Guru Granth Sahib.

The Mool Mantra is a prayer which children learn and then remember throughout their adult lives. With these words children can begin to say their own prayers at home and in the gurdwara.

A page from a nit-nem.

19

Living with the Guru Granth Sahib

"I can remember when I was very young being told to try and sit still in the worship room. When I got older though, I could have stayed there ages. It was a great feeling, everyone sitting down together and listening to the musicians and the words of the Guru Granth Sahib. The rhythm of the music and the sound of the words were so soothing. It made me feel peaceful, relaxed and happy inside. All my worries seemed to disappear and I felt very safe and comfortable listening to the Guru's word."

Have you ever tried to answer questions like 'Who created human life?' or 'Who made the world?' If you have, then your mind is already concentrating on important matters. The answer which Sikhs give to these questions is 'the True Guru, God'. Sikh children learn to meditate on God, on the teachings of the Gurus and on questions about life. They sit quietly, think and concentrate on trying to feel God's presence. Through meditation – another way to perform seva – Sikh children learn that they must love God more than themselves. Sikh children are taught that humans cannot find God on their own. They rely on the goodness of God who chooses to be close to them. This is called **nadar** – God's grace.

Make a class list of as many important questions about life as you can. Think of questions which a Sikh could answer by saying 'the True Guru, God'.

A few children are very lucky and grow up in families which have a copy of the Guru Granth Sahib at home. Children in these families have the opportunity to listen to the Guru Granth Sahib more often. They can also perform tasks such as waving the chauri over the Guru Granth Sahib. If they have learned enough Gurmukhi they can try reading small sections from the Guru Granth Sahib like a granthi. They may also use their musical instruments and sing shabads from the Guru Granth Sahib.

"I always wished that we had the Guru Granth Sahib at home like my uncle. But my dad said that we didn't have enough room. Sometimes my younger brother and I used to take the telephone directory and pretend that this was the Guru Granth Sahib. We carried it around the house above our heads on the best cushion. We used my bedroom as the worship room and took it in turns at being the granthi. We said shabads and prayers we had learned at home and at the gurdwara."

The photograph shows that the Guru Granth Sahib may have its own room in a house. This room is usually upstairs so people do not walk above the Guru Granth Sahib. Any room which houses the Guru Granth Sahib becomes a gurdwara. So family, friends and relatives behave there exactly as they would in a gurdwara.

The most important jobs children would have are keeping the room clean and making sure the Guru Granth Sahib is always treated respectfully.

A copy of the Guru Granth Sahib in a family home.

Worship in the gurdwara

"The nearest gurdwara was thirty-five miles away. So when I was very young we only went about once a month. I can remember when the local Town Hall was hired. Lots of people came and for a day the Town Hall became our gurdwara. Then later we bought an old warehouse and we made that into a gurdwara. Everybody worked together to make it look nice. Even before it was completely finished we went every Sunday morning."

Gurdwaras are usually open all the time during daylight hours. They provide places where people can sit and think and worship God.

In Indian villages in the Punjab many people go to the gurdwara on the first day of the month. This day is called **Sangrand**. You can read more about the calendar on page 37.

Sikhs always try to fit in with the customs and traditions of the people around them. In Muslim countries Friday is a special day. So Sikhs in these countries go to the gurdwara on Friday. In Britain very few people go to work on Sunday, so Sikhs in this country usually hold their main service on Sunday. This can be in the morning or in the evening. Times are chosen so that most people will be able to attend.

Services can last from one and a half to four hours. This depends on what the people in the community prefer. You can arrive and leave at any point during the service. But you must not disturb other people. On page 23 there is an outline of the service in the gurdwara.

A boy concentrating on the words and music in a gurdwara. Meditation is one way of performing seva (→ p. 7).

1 The Guru Granth Sahib is opened at random and a small section is read out by the Granthi.

2 If the service is in the morning the Giani reads out the **Sukhmani**. In the evening the **Rahiras** is said.

3 The main part of the service is kirtan. This is the singing of shabads from the Guru Granth Sahib. Musicians lead the **sangat** in kirtan. Everyone can join in if they want to.

4 Children or adults sometimes read Sikh poetry or tell stories from the lives of the ten Gurus.

5 Everyone says the Anand Sahib, the Song of Joy.

6 Everyone stands with their hands clasped in front of their chests. Heads are bowed slightly. The **Ardas** prayer is sung by a Sikh who has joined the **Khalsa** (⟶ page 57). Between each verse everyone says 'Vahiguru' (Wonderful Lord).

7 At the end of Ardas the sangat says 'Vahiguruji ka Khalsa, Vahiguruji ki fateh' (The Khalsa belongs to God, Victory belongs to God).

8 The Guru Granth Sahib is opened at random. A small section is read out by the Granthi. Sometimes this is explained.

9 A small amount of karah prashad is given to everyone.

10 Langar is served.

"At the end of the service we cup our hands together. Someone then comes round and gives us karah prashad. When I was young we used to go out to the front to get it."

Karah prashad

Karah prashad can be made at home or at the gurdwara. Because it is sacred food, the person who makes it must have had a bath first. Shoes must be left outside the kitchen. All the utensils, the cooker and the kitchen must be clean. Shabads from the Guru Granth Sahib must be said while the karah prashad is cooking. During the Ardas prayers in the gurdwara the karah prashad is marked with a **kirpan**. This is to bless the food. Karah prashad is special and should not be wasted.

Look back through this book and make a list of the things which happen in a gurdwara. Then make a list of all the rooms which are needed. Try to design a plan for a gurdwara in which all the activities can take place.

੧ ੳ Pictures, stories and symbols

Pictures of the Gurus

"We had a picture of Guru Nanak in the living room. It was right over the fireplace. There was no doubt in my mind that he was a true messenger from God. He always appeared very, very peaceful and calm. You could never imagine Guru Nanak being upset or angry or feeling helpless or defeated. It seemed he would never lift a finger to hurt anyone. Instead, he was always kind and giving. He was a perfect person."

"Guru Gobind Singh was like the other half of Guru Nanak. He was still very holy. But he always looked prepared to stand up and fight on the side of good against evil. He would fight for the right to freedom and worship. In battle he couldn't be defeated. He looked strong and honest and proud."

Above: Guru Nanak Dev.
Below: Guru Gobind Singh.

> Compare these two pictures. Make a list of the ways in which they support what these two people say.

Pictures of Guru Nanak and Guru Gobind Singh are found in most Sikh homes. There were ten Gurus in the early history of Sikhism. Guru Nanak was the first Guru and Guru Gobind Singh was the tenth. Pictures make a home more attractive. These pictures, however, have another, special purpose. They help children to see what sort of people the Gurus were.

This picture shows all ten Gurus sitting down together with two followers. Now look at the dates which show when each of the Gurus lived. You can see that the picture shows an event which couldn't have happened. Yet it makes a very important point about their message and their authority.

The divine light of Nanak is the same,
The ways of life are the same,
Only the body has changed.

(Guru Granth Sahib)

The ten Gurus

The date in square brackets shows when they began to lead the Sikh community as Gurus.

Guru Nanak Dev	(1469–1539)	[1499]
Guru Angad Dev	(1504–1552)	[1539]
Guru Amar Das	(1479–1574)	[1552]
Guru Ram Das	(1534–1581)	[1574]
Guru Arjan Dev	(1563–1606)	[1581]
Guru Hargobind	(1595–1644)	[1606]
Guru Har Rai	(1630–1661)	[1644]
Guru Har Krishan	(1656–1664)	[1661]
Guru Tegh Bahadur	(1621–1675)	[1665]
Guru Gobind Singh	(1666–1708)	[1675]

1 What do you think Sikh children would say is the special purpose of this picture? Use the words of the Guru Granth Sahib to help you.
2 Make a timechart. Experiment with ways of showing the lifetime of each of the Gurus and the period when they led the Sikh community as Gurus.

Children also see pictures like these in the gurdwara. However, they are never placed near the Guru Granth Sahib. This shows that the Guru Granth Sahib is the most important teacher.

Guru Nanak

"Mum and Dad told us stories about the Gurus. We heard the stories last thing at night just before we went to sleep. My dad told the stories really well. He made them funny by putting on the voices of the people in the story. We heard lots of stories over and over again. But I still enjoyed them. Every time I heard a story again it was just as powerful and I felt just as involved. Most of the stories were about Guru Nanak. They weren't long stories. That meant the point of the story was always clear so there was no need to explain them. I can still remember all the stories now."

From their earliest years, Sikh children hear stories about the ten Gurus. These stories help children to understand the history of Sikhism. Children learn the names of the Gurus, what they did and their important teachings. Here is the story of Nanak being called to be the Guru.

One day Nanak went down to the river for a bath. He took off his clothes and plunged into the water. Suddenly he disappeared and people feared that he had drowned. The river was searched and divers were sent down to look. All hope faded away. Nanak was dead! Some people started to gossip. They said Nanak had put an end to his own life. Perhaps he had done something wrong and was frightened of being found out. At the end of the third day, Nanak reappeared. The people of Sultanpur rejoiced. But now Nanak was a changed man. Divine glory shone on his face. Crowds gathered around him. He was no longer Nanak. Instead, he was Guru Nanak, the Teacher of the World. He had come to help the millions of people who were trying to find their way in darkness. He said these words:

'There is neither Hindu nor Muslim,
So whose path shall I follow?
I shall follow God's path.
God is neither Hindu nor Muslim
And the path which I follow is God's.'

"Sometimes if we have a problem Dad tells us a story. In the story we can see ourselves. I'm amazed he knows so many stories. The stories help you to tell the difference between right and wrong, how to be a good person and avoid being bad."

It is not essential for Sikh families to have books which tell the stories of the Gurus. Sikh parents hear the stories many times during their childhood and at the gurdwara. Sometimes a story will be slightly different. The children know that the exact words of a story are not as important as its meaning.

This is another story about Guru Nanak when he was a young man, before he was called to be the Guru.

Guru Nanak's parents were becoming very worried. They thought their son would never find a proper job. His father thought he wasted too much time daydreaming. So they decided to try and interest him in business. His father gave him some money and sent him to the market. Guru Nanak went with his friend Bala to try and make a profitable bargain. On their way they saw some Hindu holy men. Guru Nanak said, 'See how weak and hungry they look. Some of them have hardly any clothes.' So at the market Guru Nanak bought some food and clothes. He gave these to the Hindu holy men.

When he got home his father ran out to meet him. He called out, 'How did you get on? How much money did you make?' When Nanak told him what he had done with the money his father was very angry. Nanak said, 'But I thought I made a very profitable bargain'.

See if you can say what the meaning of the story would be to a Sikh child. Write down your ideas and then discuss them in small groups.

"The stories I heard made me into a Sikh. I don't follow the Gurus by thinking 'What would Guru Nanak do in this situation?' I want to copy the Gurus, but they are perfect people. I can only be like a shadow."

Children learn that the Gurus were perfect from birth. Even so, Sikhs do not worship the Gurus. They are only human beings, not God.

Guru Gobind Singh

"Dad used to buy books and comics for us to read. The stories of Guru Gobind Singh were really inspiring. He fought against evil without losing his honour. When most people fight they lose something of themselves. Guru Gobind Singh never lost anything of his person."

Children hear many stories about Guru Gobind Singh. Most of these stories are about his battles with the Muslim governors of India and the Emperor, Aurangzeb. Guru Gobind Singh's father and many other Sikhs had been executed because they refused to become Muslims. Guru Gobind Singh realised that he must fight for the freedom of both Sikhs and Hindus. Children can see that Guru Gobind Singh used the sword only when there was no alternative.

The Muslim rulers of India were the mightiest power in the whole of the Indian subcontinent. But Guru Gobind Singh was not afraid. 'I will teach the sparrow to hunt the hawk', he said.

In 1699 Guru Gobind Singh asked his Sikhs to assemble at Anandpur Sahib on the first day of Baisakh (⟶ page 36).

Here is the story of that important meeting. It is taken from a comic for Sikh children.

---

1 Either write a letter from one of the **Panj Piare** to a friend, or make a tape recording, describing what happened.
2 Make a list of all the things a Sikh child would learn about the qualities a true Sikh should show.

GURU TOOK THE SIKH INTO HIS TENT WHERE
GOATS HAD BEEN TIED UP.

THEN GURU GOBIND WENT BACK INTO THE TENT AND BROUGHT OUT THE
FIVE SIKHS — ALIVE. THEY WERE DRESSED IN NEW CLOTHES AND FINE
WEAPONS SO THAT THEY LOOKED LIKE THE GURU.

WHEN THE GURU REAPPEARED, HE WAS ALONE AND HIS SWORD WAS STAINED RED WITH BLOOD.

I WANT FOUR MORE HEADS TO OFFER AS A SACRIFICE TO GOD.

SAME HAPPENED WITH FOUR OTHER SIKHS
O OFFERED THEIR LIVES TO GOD.

THESE ARE MY BELOVED FIVE — MY PANJ PIARE. MANY MORE OF YOU WANTED TO OFFER YOUR LIVES TO GOD BUT I WANTED ONLY FIVE. THEY ARE THE BEGINNING OF A NEW COMMUNITY — THE KHALSA.

THEY ARE ALL ALIVE! BUT HOW WAS HIS SWORD DRIPPING WITH BLOOD?

THE GURU WAS TESTING OUR FAITH IN GOD!

TER ON, GURU GOBIND ASKED FOR A STEEL BOWL WHICH
FILLED WITH WATER. HIS WIFE ADDED SUGAR CRYSTALS TO
WATER. WHILE SAYING PRAYERS, THE GURU STIRRED THE
TURE WITH A DOUBLE-EDGED SWORD.
N THE PANJ PIARE WERE GIVEN THIS AMRIT.

GURU GOBIND TOLD THE KHALSA THAT THEY MUST NEVER
HARM THE WEAK AND SHOULD THINK OF ALL PEOPLE AS
BELONGING TO THE SAME FAMILY.

FROM NOW ON EACH OF YOU WILL BE CALLED SINGH. YOU WILL GROW YOUR HAIR AND BEARD, CARRY A KANGHA AND A KIRPAN, WEAR A KARA AND THE KACHH.

N4 OTHERS TOOK
RIT THAT DAY.

THE NAME KAUR WAS GIVEN TO WOMEN AND GIRLS.

JUST AS WE HAVE TAKEN AMRIT, WE MUST ALSO GIVE IT TO YOU. YOU WILL NO LONGER BE GURU GOBIND RAI, BUT GURU GOBIND SINGH.

SO BE IT. THE GURU IS OF THE KHALSA AS MUCH AS THE KHALSA IS OF THE GURU.

Kes and kangha

"Nobody had to explain why we wear the five Ks. We just know because we've heard the story of the Khalsa many times. The story says that we must be different from other people. We must be seen as Sikhs. It also says that we must stand together as Sikhs."

Sikhs follow Guru Gobind Singh by wearing the five Ks. When children are very young parents will never cut their child's hair or visit the hairdresser. As they grow up, children must decide for themselves to follow the Guru's teaching.

In Punjabi the five Ks are called the 'panj **kakke**'. In Gurmukhi script the panj kakke look like this:

ਕੇਸ

ਕੰਘਾ

ਕ੍ਰਿਪਾਨ

ਕੜਾ

ਕਛ

> Try saying the names of the panj kakke in Punjabi.

Kes

"My friends say my hair is really long and beautiful. They are always asking me how long it takes to wash and comb it. When they ask how long it took me to grow it I say, 'All my life'. They don't know what to say to that. Sometimes I do get a bit fed up with it. It takes so long to comb because it gets so many knots in. I don't want to cut it though because I'll lose something of myself. Everyone would be the same. I want to be different."

All the Sikh Gurus kept their hair long and had a beard. The Gurus taught that hair is a gift from God. So it should not be cut. It shows that a Sikh loves God and follows God's teaching. It is also a sign of strength in a man and a sign of beauty in a woman.

The **kes** must be properly cared for. It has to be combed at least twice a day and washed regularly. It is a serious offence to let hair become untidy or unclean.

"When I was young I sometimes used to ask my dad if I could have my hair cut. I wanted to be like everyone else at school. He just said, 'OK, let's go to the hairdressers'. That made me think and so I'd tell him that I didn't really mean it. Once I heard the story of Bhai Taru Singh. I felt then that I would be letting my ancestors down if I cut my hair."

In 1742 a man called Bhai Taru Singh was dragged before the Muslim authorities. His only crime was that he was a Sikh. He was given the choice of giving up Sikhism or death. Bhai Taru Singh chose death. His executioners wanted to cut off his hair first to humiliate him. Bhai Taru Singh protested saying that he would only allow his scalp to be taken off. This would leave his kes intact. While he was being put to death Bhai Taru Singh continued to recite the Sikh Morning Prayer.

Kangha

To help keep the hair clean and tidy Sikh children must also carry a comb or **kangha**. A boy ties his hair neatly in a top-knot or **jura** on top of his head. The comb is then tucked under the jura. This way it is ready for use all the time. A girl wears her hair loose or tied back in a plait or pony tail. The kangha is then tucked underneath the hair or carried in a pocket.

Children inside the gurdwara. See if you can name the different types of headcoverings (→ p. 32).

Tying a turban

Very small boys sometimes wear their hair in two plaits. These are coiled and pinned to the back of the head. As they get older it is important for boys to wear some kind of headcovering. This makes sure the kes is properly cared for.

At first, they might wear a small handkerchief or **rumal** over the jura. This is fixed in place with an elastic band or a piece of string around the jura.

A **patka** is a larger headcovering. It is a square piece of muslin which has four tapes of the same material on each corner. The tapes are used to wrap around the head and tie around the jura.

"I first learned to tie my own turban when I was about eight. My father taught me. He showed me a few times. I also used to watch my older brother tying his turban. It was difficult in the beginning. I stood in front of a mirror and tied it. Then I'd take it off and start again. Once you learn how to tie a turban it's very easy. My mother was really pleased when I could tie my own turban. She bought me four more lengths of cloth in different colours. Not everyone starts wearing a turban at the same age. It's a very personal matter, you decide what's best for you. My cousin is fourteen and he still doesn't wear a turban."

The turban is not one of the panj kakke. Children learn that all the Gurus wore turbans so Sikhs too should wear turbans. By doing this they are following the Gurus as closely as possible. At one time, only religious teachers or important people with responsibility wore turbans in India. So a Sikh turban shows that all Sikhs are religious people, each person is equally important and all Sikhs are responsible for others as well as themselves.

A turban is a piece of unsewn cotton or muslin. It is about five metres long and one metre wide and it is very light in weight. Sikhs can choose what colour turban they want to wear, although older men tend to wear blue or white. In India a turban helps to keep the head cool in summer and warm in winter. It is not put on and taken off like a hat. It should not be ready-made. It should be tied each morning and washed at least once a week.

There are several Punjabi names for the turban. Children learn that it can be called a **dastar**, a **pag**, a **pagri** or, for a large turban, a **pagra**. They will also know Punjabi expressions which mention

The combed hair is twisted into a plait.

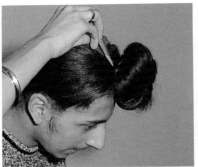
The hair is fixed in place with a kangha.

The cloth is wound around the head. One end is held in the teeth.

The turban is laid evenly and pulled tight.

The last bit of cloth is tucked into the top of the turban and covers the hair.

The turban completely tied.

turbans. These suggest how special the turban is: 'You've disgraced your turban' means you have done something wrong. 'You've knocked his turban off' means you have insulted someone. 'You deserve your turban' means you have made a good decision or behaved well.

Sardarji, which means 'chief', is a title of respect for a man who wears kes and a turban. Indian children of all religions learn to address a Sikh man whose name they do not know as 'sardarji'.

"My grandad told me that at one time in India you could tell where a man came from by the style of his turban. There were different styles for each area of the Punjab."

Make up an interview between a Sikh and a non-Sikh. In the interview, the Sikh should describe the turban and explain its importance.

Kirpan, kara and kachh

Kirpan

*"I've always worn a **kirpan** or sword. It's about the size of a pen. I wear it on a strap which goes over my right shoulder and across my chest. My kirpan hangs on the left at my waist. As children we never played around with the kirpan. We knew it was there for a special purpose. It shows that we are prepared to fight in self-defence just like Guru Gobind Singh. It also shows that we would stand up for other people who are not strong enough to fight for themselves. Fighting can mean all sorts of things. It can be speaking out for someone or just helping them when things get difficult."*

This person must be right-handed. If a person is left-handed then the kirpan is placed on the right. That way it is always ready for use.

Many children and some adults carry a very small kirpan. This might be on a chain around the neck or on a brooch. Sometimes it might be set into one side of the kangha.

A boy with a kirpan. Notice the kara on his right hand.

Kara

*"I think ever since I was born I've worn a **kara**. When it gets too small I buy another one. I put the new one on before I take the old one off. The kara belongs to the Guru. It's like a chain around your hand. It says that you are a servant of the Guru. Whenever I use my hands, the kara is always there. It reminds me that I belong to somebody and that I should behave as the Gurus would want me to."*

The kara is a ring of steel which is worn like a bangle on the wrist. It is worn on the hand that will use the kirpan. This way it protects the hand that uses the kirpan. It also reminds Sikh children that the kirpan must be used only for good purposes.

The kara should not be made of gold or silver. Steel is much stronger and it is much cheaper. Its strength suggests the strength of the Sikh community and, since everyone can afford a steel kara, it also symbolises equality. Most symbols have several layers of meaning, and one of the other meanings of the kara is that the complete circle stands for the oneness of God and of the Sikh community. The circle which has no beginning or end also represents the never-ending God.

Kachh

The **kachh**, sometimes also called **kachhahira**, are cotton shorts worn as underwear. In the time of Guru Gobind Singh they would have been part of a soldier's dress. They are designed to allow freedom of movement. The traditional Indian clothing for men is a long cloth called a dhoti. It is very difficult to run or fight in a dhoti. So the kachh symbolise that a Sikh should be prepared and active in all situations.

---

1 Draw pictures of the panj kakke and label them in Gurmukhi and with the transliteration. Then make a list of all the things they would remind Sikh children of.

2 In this book there are other Sikh symbols. As you find them, you can make a 'collection' of all the Sikh symbols and their meanings.

Most Sikh children wear the panj kakke. When they are older they might choose to make firmer promises and decide they want to take amrit and join the 'Pure Ones' or Khalsa (⟶ page 57).

Times and places

Baisakhi

"We put on our best clothes on the morning of Baisakhi and go to the gurdwara. In the gurdwara there are all sorts of special events which last all day. We sing shabads and sometimes special people come to entertain us. They tell us about Baisakhi day and why it is important to us. Everyone receives karah prashad and eats in the langar."

Baisakhi is a festival celebrated by many people in India, but Sikhs celebrate it to remember the important event which took place on the first day of Baisakh in 1699 (—→ page 28). Some children tell the story of the Panj Piare in the gurdwara. Others sing songs or tell stories about the famous battles of Guru Gobind Singh. Everyone learns that Baisakhi in 1699 was the beginning of Sikh freedom. On that day the Khalsa was created.

During the day the flag and flag-pole outside the gurdwara are taken down and the flag-pole is carefully washed in milk and yoghurt. Anyone can take part in washing the flag-pole. Often there are so many people there that it is difficult to get a very good view.

Nishan sahib

The flag is called the **nishan sahib** and it flies above every gurdwara. It is made of saffron cloth and the flagpole is covered with the same kind of cloth. In the middle of the flag is the **khanda** emblem. The actual khanda is the two-edged sword in the centre. This symbolises that there is one God and he is concerned with truth and justice. The circle, or **chakar**, represents the one, never-ending God. The two kirpans symbolise God's power over both this world and the spiritual world.

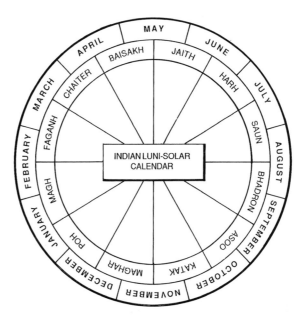

The calendar

According to the ancient Indian calendar, Baisakhi was the first day of the New Year. The year started with the month of Baisakh. On the western calendar this is April 13. Sometimes, however, it changes to April 14. It did this in 1975, 1983 and 1987. Baisakhi day is fixed by the movement of the sun. Sikhs also use another calendar with months based on the movement of the moon. A lunar year is shorter than a solar year, so the lunar calendar is adjusted regularly. This way, it stays in line with the solar calendar. Because the calendar uses both the moon and the sun it is called a luni-solar calendar. You can see from this diagram that the months of the luni-solar calendar do not match the months of the western calendar. Every year, according to the movement of the moon, the lunar months can move by about fifteen days. This means that the first day of Faganh can fall either in the middle of February or at the beginning of March. All the other Sikh festivals are celebrated according to the luni-solar calendar so they move about slightly from year to year.

1 Make a copy of the calendar. Mark on it the festival of Baisakhi.
2 Write a letter to a non-Sikh friend describing what happens at Baisakhi and explaining what it means to Sikhs.
3 Read what happened in Amritsar on Baisakhi in 1919 (⟶ page 56). Write an article for a Punjabi newspaper describing the events.

Hola Mohalla

"When I was young I lived in a small village in the Punjab. On the morning of Hola Mohalla we went to the gurdwara. We were really excited because the fun fair was outside and there were lots of shops and stalls there as well.

Later on there were all sorts of contests. There were fencing, wrestling, hockey and horse racing competitions. We even had a game of tug-o-war. Each family had to organise a team. That was great fun. We also played Punjabi team games like **kabadi** *and* **sat pathar***. At the end of the day we sometimes went back to the gurdwara to thank God for our health and strength. In Britain, Hola Mohalla is much quieter, although it seems to be getting better each year."*

Some of the games that children play both at Hola Mohalla and throughout the year are known across the world. However, Sikh children who grow up in India learn many more traditional Punjabi games than they do in Britain. Sat pathar is a very popular game with boys and girls in the Punjab. The name means 'seven stones'. There are different names for this game and different ways to play it. Here is one set of rules. See if it reminds you of any games you play.

Sat pathar

1 You need a soft tennis ball and seven stones.
   Form two teams of two, three or four people. One team is 'throwing' (Team A), the other is 'fielding' (Team B).

2 Make a pile of the seven stones.

3 Team A throw the ball to try and knock down the pile of stones.

4 When they succeed they must rebuild the pile as quickly as possible.

5 Team B run for the ball and throw it so it hits one of Team A before they rebuild the pile. If they succeed then Team A are out and they become 'fielders'.

6 If Team A rebuild the pile then they score a point and continue to throw the ball.

A game of kabadi at a sports stadium. Kabadi involves the strength and speed needed in the game of 'bulldog'.

Hola Mohalla is on the day following a very ancient Hindu festival called Holi. But Guru Gobind Singh wanted the Sikhs to be together as a community rather than joining in with Hindu celebrations. So in 1700 he called everyone to the town of Anandpur Sahib for Holi. Guru Gobind Singh decided that for a few days he would train his army. The name 'Hola Mohalla' means 'tactical manoeuvres'. The Sikh army performed mock battles and contests. They even attacked a fortress which was specially built for the occasion. Guru Gobind Singh also organised poetry, music and sports competitions.

Today many Sikh families who are in India go to the fair at Anandpur Sahib to see the contests and displays. At the end of the festival there is a parade of nishan sahibs. Hola Mohalla is a celebration of health and freedom.

"Hola Mohalla is rather different in places where there are lots of Sikhs and Hindus living together. In these places people tend to follow the Hindu customs and traditions. Everyone wears old clothes and throws coloured powder and water at each other. It's great when everyone joins together, even though they are celebrating different things."

Hola Mohalla is celebrated in the month of Faganh. Mark it in on your calendar.

Divali

Fireworks, candles and sweets make Divali a very popular festival with Sikh children.

"In India, I knew months before when Divali was coming. I looked forward to it because we got the day off from school every year. I used to start counting the days to Divali on the calendar. My mum bought the fireworks and divided them equally between me and my three brothers. Just before Divali everyone helped to paint the whole house.

On Divali morning, we dressed in our best clothes and went to the gurdwara to pray. During the day we helped Mum to cook food and sweets. We seemed to eat sweets all day! When we weren't helping we played outside.

The best part happened at night. We lit candles all round the house. Then we climbed on to the flat rooftop. It was really beautiful. When you looked round at all the houses it seemed as though the stars had fallen to the ground.

Everybody had their own firework display with families and friends. We all lit our own fireworks. They made an incredible noise! The celebrations finished at about eleven o'clock. When it was over I could only think about how long it was to the next Divali night."

Children celebrating Divali with sparklers. Colourful clothes are often worn at Divali.

Hindus also celebrate Divali, but Sikhs have given the festival its own new meaning. One of the stories Sikh children hear explains why it is celebrated.

Hargobind became the sixth Guru after his father, Guru Arjan Dev, had been tortured to death by the Muslim emperor. The same Muslim governor arrested Guru Hargobind on charges of plotting against the Emperor. He also accused the Guru of failing to pay a large fine which his father owed to the authorities. Guru Hargobind was imprisoned at Gwalior Fort with fifty-two Hindu princes. Two years later Emperor Jehangir found out that the Guru was in prison. He examined the charges, knew the Guru was innocent, and ordered his immediate release. Guru Hargobind refused to leave unless the Hindu princes were also set free. The Emperor said that the Guru could take with him all those who could hold on to his clothing as he passed through a narrow passage. The Guru sent for a cloak which had long tassles along the edges. By holding on to these tassles, all the Hindu princes were set free with Guru Hargobind.

The Guru headed straight for Amritsar. When news of his arrival reached the city the Sikhs lit candles around their houses as a sign of celebration.

Sikh children everywhere celebrate Divali. They help to decorate their houses or the gurdwara with fairy lights and candles. These lights are to remember the return of Guru Hargobind. But they also remind children that just as the light of candles conquers darkness, so the voice of the True Guru ends the darkness of ignorance.

"In Britain, we all take boxes of sweets to the gurdwara to share with our friends. There are candles everywhere, both inside and outside the gurdwara. It looks very beautiful. Sometimes it's like a competition to see who can bring the biggest candle! Most of the cards we send in this country have small lamps – devas – on the front. They're the same as the cards that Hindus send at Divali. I don't think I've ever seen a Sikh Divali card. One year I got a card from my Hindu friend. That was nice."

---

1 Divali is celebrated in the month of Katak. Mark in the festival on your calendar.
2 Design a card which would be appropriate to send to a Sikh friend at Divali. You could use some of the symbols and Gurmukhi script from this book.
3 Make a wall display showing all the things which happen at Divali.

Days for the Gurus

Sikh children also join in festivals in which they remember the birthdays or the deaths of the ten Gurus. These occasions are called **gurpurbs**, which means 'holy days of the Guru'.

"Two days before a gurpurb we start the celebrations in the gurdwara. From early in the morning, after prayers, Granthis take it in turns to read through the whole Guru Granth Sahib. It takes about forty-eight hours and finishes on the morning of the gurpurb. We can go to listen to the reading whenever we like. Everyone tries to go to the gurdwara on the morning of the gurpurb to listen to the last part of the Guru Granth Sahib. Then we have kirtan and listen to stories and talks about the Guru whose gurpurb we are celebrating. With so many people there the langar is very busy. Sometimes there are competitions and sports afterwards."

Akhand path

The non-stop reading of the whole Guru Granth Sahib is called an **akhand path**. Before an akhand path starts karah prashad is prepared, six verses of the Anand Sahib are read, the Ardas prayer is offered and a blessing is asked for the reading. The Guru Granth Sahib is then opened at random and a short piece is read. Then the akhand path starts. Each Granthi reads for no more than two hours at a time and there is always another Granthi ready to take over during a reading. Someone else must also be there to give karah prashad to people who come to listen to the akhand path.

Celebrating the Gurus with an akhand path teaches children that the Guru Granth Sahib is the best way to understand the lives and teachings of the ten Gurus. It also reminds them that the Guru Granth Sahib can lead them to the True Guru, God.

There are four main gurpurbs which are remembered by Sikhs everywhere:

1 The birthday of Guru Nanak (in Katak).
2 The birthday of Guru Gobind Singh (in Poh).
3 The martyrdom of Guru Arjan Dev (in Jaith).
4 The martyrdom of Guru Tegh Bahadur (in Maghar).

The birthdays of the other Gurus are celebrated every year in the places where they were born and by all Sikhs in centenary and half-centenary years.

Sikh children hear the stories of the martyrdoms of Guru Arjan Dev and Guru Tegh Bahadur as they grow up. They are stories with an important message.

The torture of Guru Arjan Dev

The Emperor Jehangir became very concerned at the increasing influence of Guru Arjan Dev. So he had him arrested and imprisoned. The Emperor agreed to free him only if he became a Muslim. Guru Arjan Dev refused and was sentenced to death by torture. He was made to sit on a burning hot plate, boiled alive and then drowned in a river. Throughout this cruel torture the Guru did not change his mind.

The sacrifice of Guru Tegh Bahadur

A group of Hindus visited Guru Tegh Bahadur. They said that Emperor Aurangzeb had threatened the Hindu community with death unless they all became Muslims. The Guru said that they should agree to become Muslims only if he could be converted first. Guru Tegh Bahadur was called before the Emperor. He was told all the advantages of becoming a Muslim. He refused to change. His two followers were executed in front of him. But he still refused. Then he was sentenced to death. Guru Tegh Bahadur said the Morning Prayer and was then beheaded.

1 Work out which years will be centenary and half-centenary gurpurbs for the births of the Gurus (⟶ page 25).
2 Can you explain why some Sikhs celebrate Baisakhi as a gurpurb (⟶ page 36)?
3 Can you explain what meaning the two stories in this chapter might have for Sikh children?

In India children join in street parades to celebrate gurpurbs. The Guru Granth Sahib is carried on a float surrounded by flowers. At the front are five Sikhs who represent the Panj Piare. Shabads are sung and people shout out 'sat shri akal' (⟶ page 18).

Journeys

Sikh children learn that there is one 'journey' which must be made in life. This is a journey of the spirit. It is to explore yourself and the meaning of life. On page 20 you read that part of this journey is made by meditating on important questions. Children also say the words 'Vahiguru' and '**Nam**' in their minds to help them on this journey. 'Nam' means 'name', the name of the True Guru, God, who fills the universe. With God's grace the journey leads to the feeling that everything lives within God.

Sikh children and their families often make other journeys – pilgrimages – to places in India. There are many famous gurdwaras in the Punjab which are reminders of the lives of the Gurus. It is not essential to visit these places, but many children find it a very special experience.

*"I was twelve when I first saw the **Darbar Sahib**. It was much better than the pictures I'd seen at home and in the gurdwara. It was so big and so beautiful. I was used to going to a small gurdwara where you did some work in the langar and listened to shabads. There were many rooms at the Darbar Sahib and so much was going on. First of all, we walked all the way round the pool. Then we went across the bridge into the temple. Inside, a Granthi was reading the Guru Granth Sahib. We walked round behind the Guru Granth Sahib very slowly. You completely forget about everything outside and it gives you real peace in your mind. After receiving karah prashad we bathed in the pool and then ate in the langar.*

We stayed up all that night. Early in the morning, at about three o'clock, the Guru Granth Sahib was carried from a building called the Akhal Takht Sahib to the temple in the middle. It's only about two hundred yards but it took nearly half an hour. I walked behind all the way. The Darbar Sahib made me feel good inside and proud to be a Sikh."

The Golden Temple

Guru Ram Das built the city of Amritsar and excavated the pool which now surrounds the Darbar Sahib – the Golden Temple. Amritsar is named after this man-made pool. The name means 'pool of nectar'. In 1589 Guru Arjan Dev asked a Muslim, Mian Mir, to lay the foundations of the gurdwara in the centre of the pool. It was built with four doors to show that people of all religions are welcome to visit. One of the first copies of the Adi Granth was placed inside. The original building was destroyed in

The Golden Temple or Darbar Sahib at Amritsar.

1757 and later rebuilt by Maharajah Ranjit Singh in white marble. He covered the top half and the domes of the four towers in gold leaf.

Inside the Darbar Sahib kirtan is continuous from three o'clock in the morning until late at night. On the upper floor of the Darbar Sahib the Guru Granth Sahib is read. At night it is placed in a silver box and carried in a procession to a building at the side of the pool, the Akhal Takht Sahib. The other buildings which surround the Darbar Sahib are a library, a museum and the langar. The langar serves food twenty-four hours a day to all visitors.

Copy the map on page 56. Use an atlas to find these important sites: Amritsar, Anandpur Sahib, Nanakana Sahib, Kartarpur Sahib and Goindwal, and mark them on your map. Find out from this book, and any other sources, why there are special gurdwaras in these places.

45

 # Belonging

A new baby

"Mum and Dad both wanted a baby boy because they already had two daughters. My sister and I also thought a brother would be great fun. We'd be able to play with him and look after him. When Mum was expecting the baby we brought a Guru Granth Sahib home. We placed it in the spare room upstairs. Mum, Dad and some of their friends read through the whole Guru Granth Sahib. Because it wasn't read continuously it took about ten days. Every evening all the family came together to pray and to listen to the Guru Granth Sahib. We all hoped that the baby would be a boy. If it was a girl we wouldn't have been disappointed because God knows best what our family needs."

Expecting a baby is always an exciting event for a family. Families are joined together by their hopes and thoughts about what the baby and the new family will be like. By praying together, Sikh families show that they are grateful to God for the baby which will soon be with them. You can see that even before the baby is born it is already part of a Sikh family.

Sahaj path

Some Sikh families share their happiness and hopes by reading all the Guru Granth Sahib at home. This is called a **sahaj path**. It is the same as an akhand path (→ page 42) except that the reading is not continuous. This means that the Guru Granth Sahib can be read at times when most of the family are together. All the family will be present for the reading of the last part of the Guru Granth Sahib, which cannot be interrupted. A sahaj path can be held at times of happiness, sadness and hope. It shows children that the Guru Granth Sahib is the centre of their family life.

The Gurus showed that families and children were important by their examples. Each of the ten Gurus, except Guru Har Krishan, was married and had children. One story even tells how Guru Angad kept the Emperor of India, Humayun, waiting while he played games with the children in his village.

Choosing a name

"We were really excited when we got a baby brother. When he came home from hospital we all got dressed in our best clothes and took him to the gurdwara. Lots of our friends and relatives came along as well. Going to the gurdwara was like saying 'thank you' to God. It was very special because the baby was a boy – just what we'd all been hoping for. After prayers, the Guru Granth Sahib was opened at random. The first letter of the shabad on the left-hand page was a 'g'. My parents had to say then and there what his name was. They chose 'Gurpreet'. This is much better than just going home and thinking of a name. It shows you are grateful to God."

A new baby is taken to the gurdwara as soon as possible. Usually, this is to the main service of worship. Special shabads are sung during kirtan. One of them was composed by Guru Arjan Dev on the birth of his son, Guru Hargobind. After kirtan, the Anand Sahib and the Ardas prayer are said. Then the Guru Granth Sahib is opened, a short section is read out, and the name is chosen for the baby. Sometimes friends and relatives help by suggesting names to the parents. When the name has been chosen, the Granthi announces it to the whole congregation, adding either **'Singh'** for a boy or **'Kaur'** for a girl. Everyone shows they accept the name by saying, 'sat shri akal' (→ page 18). Karah prashad is then given to everyone.

All Sikh children know that their first name was chosen by opening the Guru Granth Sahib and using the first letter of the shabad at the top of the left-hand page. This shows them that from the beginning, the Guru Granth Sahib is the centre of their lives.

Singh and Kaur

Nearly all Sikh names can be used for both boys and girls. This is why it is often important to use the second names 'Singh' and 'Kaur'. Most Sikh children grow up with these surnames, sometimes in addition to family names. They can be used by all Sikhs, not just those who have joined the Khalsa (⟶ pages 29, 57). Guru Gobind Singh asked Sikhs to use these names to show that everyone belongs to the same family or community.

---

1 First names can begin with any of the letters of the Gurmukhi script. Here are some Gurmukhi characters and some transliterated names. Copy out the list of names and write out beside each name the Gurmukhi letter with which the name starts.

ਤ ਪ ਰ ਸ
ਹ ਕ ਜ ਮ
ਗ ਬ

Surjinder	Jaswant
Mandeep	Kamaljeet
Pritpal	Balinder
Ranjeet	Daljeet
Gurinder	Harminder

2 Now write the names in Gurmukhi script.

3 From this book, and other sources, make a list of as many Sikh first names as you can.

It is a traditional custom for Sikh parents to give presents on the birth of a baby. They often take karah prashad to the gurdwara and a new rumala for the Guru Granth Sahib to show that they are grateful to God for their baby. The baby is also part of a family of many relatives, so parents share their happiness by giving them presents of sweets and new clothes. In return, the baby and its parents receive many gifts. As well as giving sweets, it is usual to give the father a new turban or shirt and the mother a new sari or **salwar kameez** (⟶ page 51). Like all babies, a Sikh baby receives lots of clothes and toys.

Many Sikh parents also ask for another ceremony for their baby. The Granthi prepares amrit in a small metal bowl while saying the first five verses of the **Japji Sahib**. Amrit is made in the same way as Guru Gobind Singh first made it on Baisakhi in 1699 (→ page 29). The tip of a kirpan is dipped into the amrit and then the baby's tongue is touched with it. Afterwards, the mother drinks the rest of the amrit. Then the name is chosen using the Guru Granth Sahib. Giving amrit to a baby is a way of showing that the baby is part of a larger family – the community of Sikhs.

The community

Sikh children are introduced to the community as soon as possible. You read on page 47 how a baby's name is chosen and then announced to everyone in the gurdwara. Sometimes parents arrange for another way in which to show their gratitude to God and to introduce their baby to the community.

"A few weeks after my brother was born Mum and Dad organised an akhand path at the gurdwara. We spent a long time there. It's very impolite to ask for an akhand path and not to go along. My dad did some of the reading from the Guru Granth Sahib. Lots of people came along and by the end everyone knew my brother and his name."

The community is where Sikh children make many of their friends. As they grow up they may join youth groups organised by the gurdwara. These groups are usually for sports. Hockey and table tennis are two games which are very popular in the Punjab and with Sikh children in Britain.

Older people also take an interest in how children are growing up. Most people in the Sikh community share the same beliefs about God, mankind, the Guru Granth Sahib and the teachings of the Gurus. So the community is the place which will help children to learn about their religion. It will also help them to know what it means to be a Sikh.

A karate lesson organised by a gurdwara.

49

Women and girls

Dressing in the same way as adults helps children to feel part of a community. It shows that you belong to a group of people. Sikh children wear the panj kakke and one day boys will also wear turbans. Girls and women dress in a certain style as well. They don't have to wear these clothes, but, like the turban, they are part of belonging to a community. This girl explains why she wears these clothes and describes what her favourite salwar kameez looks like.

"I wear English clothes all the time except when I go to the gurdwara. I like to wear salwar kameez because then you're not the odd one out. Besides, they're very comfortable to wear. My mum made my best salwar kameez. The kameez is like a shirt. This one is bright yellow with buttons down the side. That's the fashion now. The salwar are the trousers. Mine are yellow to match the kameez. They've got small patterns on in silver and there are red, green and blue squares all over. They're called 'dhoti salwar' because they're baggy. The **chuni** *is also yellow with silver threads woven in. When Mum had finished them I couldn't wait to go to the gurdwara."*

In India most Sikh girls and women wear these clothes all the time. They are traditional Punjabi dress. In other areas of India most women wear a sari. There is nothing to stop Sikh women wearing a sari. But, like men, they must make sure they are properly dressed, so the sari top should cover their waist and stomach.

> The opposite page shows three styles of salwar kameez. Design a salwar kameez using cloth, coloured paper or colouring pens. If you are particularly skilled you could dress a doll in salwar kameez. Look through this book for ideas on styles and colours. Your class could design a whole range of outfits for your final display.

"Our Religious Studies teacher visited the gurdwara with a group from school. I didn't know they were coming. I was wearing my salwar kameez. They hadn't seen it before but they thought it was really nice."

"Apart from the clothes we wear, boys and girls are equal. We all have to do the same things and we can all join in when we want to. When I was young we heard many stories about Sikh women. Most of them were about Guru Nanak's sister, **Bibi** Nanaki. She was the first person to understand Guru Nanak for what he was. We also heard about the many brave women who worked and struggled for Sikhism."

The stories children hear show that women can share in the personal qualities of both Guru Nanak and Guru Gobind Singh ($\longrightarrow$ page 24).

Bibi Nanaki was Guru Nanak's only sister. From when he was very young she recognized that Guru Nanak had been chosen by God. When their father criticised Nanak for not learning a trade she defended him. She invited Nanak to leave their home town of Talvandi (later renamed Nanakana Sahib) to live with her in Sultanpur. It was there that Nanak disappeared in the river for three days. When other people said that Nanak was dead, Bibi Nanaki replied, 'The sun will set only after flooding everyone with light'.

Guru Gobind Singh and his followers were surrounded by the Muslim army at Anandpur Sahib. Soon there were only about a hundred people left to defend the Guru. The Muslim commanders promised freedom to all those Sikhs who surrendered. A group of forty Sikhs tried to persuade Guru Gobind Singh to accept the offer. He refused. The forty then rejected the Guru and left for home.

Soon they reached their villages. However, their wives, led by Mai Bhago, told them they were cowards and urged them to return to help the Guru. Mai Bhago commanded them in battle against the Muslim army at Khidrana. When the Guru reached the battlefield only one of the forty men was alive. The Guru forgave him and blessed the others who had left him at Anandpur Sahib. Mai Bhago lived a long time after the battle. There she had helped the men to follow and support the Guru.

There are many ways in which Sikhism shows that men and women are equal. Since the beginning of Sikhism both men and women have had the right to join in discussions about the community. They also share the right to elect members on to the committees which run the gurdwaras. Start a list with these two examples. Add other examples from this book which show that in Sikhism men and women are equal.

Marriage

"We got up really early and put on our best clothes to go to the gurdwara. It was about nine o'clock when we got there. Most weddings take place in the morning and you have to be early to get a good position. Then you can be sure to see what the bride looks like in her clothes and jewellery. The groom sits at the front and the bride is at the back of the room. All the women look after her. They straighten her clothes and make sure that she

isn't too nervous. After shabads and a talk about marriage, the bride and groom walk round the Guru Granth Sahib four times. Each time it gets more exciting, because when they finish they're actually married. On the last time round everyone throws flower petals over them.''

The best parts of a wedding for this Sikh child are seeing what people wear, watching what they do and waiting for the times when everyone can join in. The presence of friends and relatives adds to the excitement. And, if it is a relative who is getting married, then there will be many more new people to get to know.

In the Punjab, it is Sikh custom for weddings to take place at the bride's home. In Britain, it is likely to be at a nearby gurdwara. This is because so many people attend weddings that it is difficult to find somewhere large enough for them all. The wedding can take place on any day of the week. Sunday is most popular in Britain because it is when most people can be present. It also means that most of the community will be there as well. Children who attend the gurdwara regularly for worship see many weddings as they grow up.

Wherever the wedding takes place, the bride always dresses in red, the colour of happiness and joy. She wears gold jewellery and sometimes her hands and feet are decorated with henna patterns. The groom can wear traditional Punjabi dress or a suit. He usually wears a brightly coloured turban as a sign of rejoicing.

The Sikh wedding ceremony is called the **anand karaj** – the ceremony of joy. Any Sikh man or woman who has been asked by the families of both the bride and groom can be in charge of the anand karaj. During the service, this person – the officiant – opens the Guru Granth Sahib and reads the verses of the **Lavan**. After each verse is read, the musicians sing it again while the couple walk clockwise round the Guru Granth Sahib.

Here is the first line from each verse of the Lavan:

The first time round for work in the world as the Guru has asked.

The second time round to recognise that God has caused you to meet the True Guru.

The third time round for the Lord and for detachment from the world.

The fourth time round for knowledge and union with God.

Anand karaj and the Lavan show children that marriage is an important stage of life. It is a way of coming closer to the True Guru, just as husband and wife come closer through marriage.

"After the wedding everybody goes to the reception. The meal is usually prepared at the gurdwara and served at the reception. When the dancing starts, everybody tries to get the bride and groom to dance together. Afterwards, they go home to the groom's house. Usually girls stand in the doorway, one holding a glass of water. They have to put some money in the glass before they can go into the house. When my sister and I did it we both had a glass each and we asked lots of guests for some money. We wanted to see who could collect the most."

"Mum and Dad have different views on who we should marry. Dad says we can choose the person we want. Mum likes the traditional wedding arrangements where they would put forward suggestions. I suppose it will be halfway between the two. I like that."

This pattern of marriage is the one which most Sikh children in Britain will grow up with. They know that they will be free to decide whether or not they wish to marry a particular person. If they do, then the two families will meet together to discuss the wedding. A wedding is more than two people making an agreement with each other. It is two families coming together.

The Punjab

"We've still got many close relatives living in the Punjab. When we go over to India we stay with them. I don't think I want to live there all the time because the lifestyle is very different. I like going there for a holiday. Once, I can remember visiting Anandpur Sahib. It's very beautiful with high mountains in the background. There's a small fortress there which I stood and looked at. I began to feel as though everything was coming to life. The stories I had heard had actually happened. It made me think about our history and how my own ancestors lived in the Punjab."

Most of the stories Sikh children hear are about events that take place in the Punjab. For children who grow up in the area it is their homeland. For Sikh children who live in other countries it is the place where the Gurus lived and where Sikhism started and grew. It is also where many of their traditions and customs come from. Sikh nursery rhymes, games, music, dancing and styles of dress all come from the Punjab. On page 38 you read about the Punjabi game sat pathar. In the Punjab, everyone plays this game, not just Sikhs. In the same way, there are other traditions, customs and stories from history which belong to everyone who comes from the Punjab. This is called Punjabi culture. It helps Sikh children to feel that they belong to a larger group of people which includes the Sikh community.

*The **bhangra** is a dance performed by men and the **gidha** a dance performed by women. The dances celebrate the harvest at Baisakhi time. Brightly coloured clothes are usually worn, sometimes with small bells tied round the ankles.*

To the Sikhs the Punjab is one land, but it was divided when the new countries of Pakistan and India were created in 1947. Some of the places where the Gurus had lived are now in India and some are in Pakistan. For example, Nanakana Sahib, where Guru Nanak was born, is now in Pakistan and Kartarpur Sahib, where Guru Arjan established a large Sikh community, is in India.

Maharajah Ranjit Singh

Sikh children hear about the time when the Punjab was one united country. It was ruled by Maharajah Ranjit Singh – the 'Lion of the Punjab'. In 1797 he brought all the Sikhs together. He captured Lahore and made it his capital. The Punjab became strong and powerful under Maharajah Ranjit Singh. The British, who were taking control of large parts of India, didn't attempt to occupy the Punjab until ten years after his death in 1839. Although he was a Sikh, most of the members of his government were Hindus and Muslims. His efficiency and fairness have made him into one of the great people in the history of the Punjab.

The name 'Punjab' means 'five rivers'. From an atlas find out the names of the five rivers which flowed through the old land of Punjab and into the River Indus. Label these on your map.

There are other events in history which give Sikhs a sense of belonging to the Punjabi community. They are landmarks in history which help Punjabi people to understand themselves and their past.

The Amritsar massacre

One event which is remembered by Punjabis everywhere occurred in 1919. A very large group of people, many of them Sikhs, met at a place called Jallianwala Bagh in Amritsar to celebrate Baisakhi. The British authorities had said that such gatherings were against the law. Because they were frightened of a rebellion a small group of soldiers were sent to Jallianwala Bagh. Without warning, they opened fire on the crowd. Some 1,650 shots were fired, several hundred people were killed and over a thousand were wounded.

PAKISTAN

Lahore • • Amritsar

R Indus

INDIA

Delhi •

The Punjab

----- International Border

Taking amrit

"One day, if I have the courage, I want to take amrit and join the Khalsa. You've got to have courage because it's a very big commitment. I'll know when the time comes because I'll feel that it's right."

The story of Baisakhi in 1699 is one which Sikh children hear many times (⟶ page 28). In the story people showed their devotion to the True Guru by taking amrit. Children know that at some point in their lives they may make the same personal decision. That decision must be as serious as the choice which the Panj Piare made when they offered their lives to the Guru.

"There are no special lessons before you take amrit. Everything that is expected of a Sikh is made clear in the gurdwara and at home from when you are small. I was eighteen when I took amrit. Early in the morning I had a bath and then dressed in traditional Sikh clothing with the panj kakke. In the gurdwara we sat as a group. This made you feel that the ceremony was going to change your life. Five people were dressed as the Panj Piare. They were ordinary people whom I knew but now they were special. I felt as though I was transported back in time. I can remember feeling a bit worried at the time about my ability to keep all the promises."

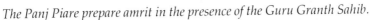

The Panj Piare prepare amrit in the presence of the Guru Granth Sahib.

Both men and women can take amrit. They can be any age but they should be old enough to have chosen to follow the Sikh way of life. The ceremony can take place in any private room. It is a personal moment and for that reason there are few people there to watch. Although Baisakhi is a very popular time for the ceremony, it can be held at any time of year.

"I've never seen anyone take amrit. But I can tell you what happens. At the beginning the Guru Granth Sahib is opened. Then one of the Panj Piare explains about Sikhism and what it means to be a Sikh. After a prayer, a passage is read from the Guru Granth Sahib. While this is happening the Panj Piare kneel, like soldiers, on their right knees round a large steel bowl and prepare the amrit. They mix together sugar and water. One by one they stir the mixture with a khanda. While they're doing this they say shabads. This can take up to two hours. Then the people who are taking amrit come forward one at a time. They kneel like the Panj Piare. Each one says 'Vahiguruji ka Khalsa, Vahiguruji ki fateh'. Amrit is then poured into their cupped hands five times and they drink it. Then the amrit is sprinkled in their hair and eyes five times."

The Panj Piare then say the Mool Mantra five times. Each time, those who are taking amrit repeat it after the Panj Piare. The senior member of the Panj Piare gives a short talk on their responsibilities as members of the Khalsa. After this the Ardas is said and a random passage is read from the Guru Granth Sahib. The ceremony ends with everyone receiving karah prashad.

Anyone who is new to Sikhism also receives a name during the amrit ceremony, before karah prashad is given out. This is the same as choosing a name for a baby ($\longrightarrow$ page 47).

Sikh children are encouraged from their earliest years to keep the promises that are made when taking amrit. Taking amrit means that these promises become a firm code for living.

The promises made when taking amrit:

1 Never to cut your hair.
2 Never to eat meat slaughtered in the Muslim or Jewish ways.
3 Never to commit adultery.
4 Never to use tobacco.
5 Never to drink alcohol.
6 To give some of your earnings to the gurdwara for charities.
7 To rise early, take a bath and say the Japji Sahib, and other prayers.
8 To say the Rahiras in the evening and the **Sohila** before going to bed.
9 To offer the Ardas regularly.
10 To wear the panj kakke and use the name 'Singh' or 'Kaur'.

"They're not the only things we have to do. We have to go to the gurdwara regularly and perform seva and we have to have the right attitude of mind."

Not all Sikh children will choose to take amrit when they grow up. However, they should still follow the code for living. This code and all the details about living as a Sikh are contained in a manual called the Sikh **Rahit Maryada**.

The Guru Granth Sahib makes the important parts of the Sikh Rahit Maryada clear to all Sikh children.

'He who calls himself a Sikh of the True Guru
Should rise early and meditate on the Name,
In the early hours of the morning he should rise and bathe
And cleanse his soul in a tank of nectar,
And he repeats the Name the Guru taught him,
Thus he washes away the sins of his soul.'

(Guru Granth Sahib)

The believing community

Sikh children grow up in the worldwide community of Sikhs – the **Panth**. This word means 'path'. Another meaning is the beliefs, teachings and work which a Sikh must follow in life. This path was laid down by the ten Gurus to help Sikhs to find the True Guru, God.

One of the most important beliefs in Sikhism is the first line of the Mool Mantra (→ page 18). The symbol for this belief is used at the beginning of each section in this book. It says that Sikhs believe there is one God – Ik Onkar.

> Make a list of the beliefs which make up the Sikh path through life. Start with the belief in one God and at the side draw the symbol for this belief. Try to use other symbols to illustrate your list of beliefs. Include your lists and illustrations with your class display on Sikhism.

"In life we have to become good people. We should perform seva, meditate and follow our religion truthfully. We are all running in a race. Some of us are fitter and can run faster than others. But that doesn't matter. Everyone should run their best and that also means helping others in the race. God knows who makes a true effort. Only by trying our best and being ready to receive God's grace can we become one with God when we die. If we have been lazy and haven't bothered to try to find God then we must live another life again."

Sikh children know that they may have lived many times before as animals or humans. But it is only as human beings that they have the opportunity to choose to love God and come close to God. Those who take that opportunity will be free from living again and will be united with God.

Freedom, equality and tolerance

"My mum and dad never made me be a Sikh. I chose that for myself. They took me to the gurdwara when I was small and I saw what life they followed and what other people did. All around I saw Sikhs performing seva in the gurdwara, in the community and through prayer. Even now, my parents look after neighbours' children and help old people who live

near us. Others run committees and offer professional advice to people with difficulties. When I saw what Sikhism was about, I wanted to learn about it. There's no point in forcing anyone to learn something they're not interested in. They just rebel and go against it.''

You have read that freedom and equality play a large part in Sikh life. You might also remember why the Darbar Sahib has four doors – one in each direction ($\longrightarrow$ page 44). This is to do with tolerance. It is making sure that other people are also respected for their beliefs and actions. Sikh parents encourage their children to be Sikhs. But they also know that their children must decide for themselves what they wish to do. This way, children learn that equality, freedom and tolerance are important values in their own lives.

''I've read pieces from the Bible and I know quite a lot about the Hindu religion. The key to all things is knowledge. Every religion has knowledge and there is nothing wrong with learning from others. They all have one aim and that is to lead you to a good life. I was born into a Sikh family and so for me, the Guru Granth Sahib is the guide to my life.''

The word 'Sikh' means a learner, disciple or follower. This shows that the whole of life is for learning and following the teachings of the Guru. A Sikh child grows up in **Gurmat** – the correct word for Sikhism. In this way, every Sikh tries to live the life of a **Gursikh**.

The Guru Granth Sahib is carried in procession from the Akhal Takht to the Darbar Sahib.

Glossary

Words in quotation marks are the translation of the Punjabi words.

Ádi Granth 'first book', 'original book', the Guru Granth Sahib

akhánd path 'complete reading', continuous reading of the Guru Granth Sahib

ámrit 'nectar', 'water of life'

anánd karaj ceremony of joy, marriage ceremony

Anánd Sáhib Song of Joy, part of the Rahiras

Ardás 'request', prayer said at the end of worship

bajá 'harmonium'

bhai 'brother'

bhangrá men's folk dance from the Punjab

bibi 'sister'

caste group or class of people

chakár 'circle'

chanáni canopy or covering to shade from the sun

cháuri fly-whisk waved over the Guru Granth Sahib as a sign of respect

chúni, dupáta scarf worn by women on head and shoulders

Dárbar Sáhib, Harimándir Sáhib 'Lord's Court', 'God's Temple', the Golden Temple in Amritsar

Dasam Granth 'book of the tenth', the collected songs and prayers of Guru Gobind Singh

dastár 'turban'

deva 'light', lamp

giáni 'scholar', person who studies and teaches religion

gídha 'clapping hands', women's folk dance from the Punjab

gránthi reader of the Guru Granth Sahib, person who looks after a gurdwara

gurbáni 'words of the Guru' in the Guru Granth Sahib

gúrdwara 'house of the Guru', Sikh place of worship

Gúrmat the teachings and beliefs of the Gurus

Gúrmukhi alphabet used for the Punjabi language

gurpúrb a day to remember an event in the life of a Guru

Gursíkh 'follower of the Guru', a true Sikh

gúru religious teacher

Gúru Granth Sáhib Sikh holy book

gútka 'manual', 'handbook' of songs and prayers from the Guru Granth Sahib and the Dasam Granth.

Japji Sahib prayer which starts with the Mool Mantra

jóri 'pair' of drums

kabádi a team game of physical strength from the Punjab

káchh/káchhahira 'shorts', 'underwear', one of the panj kakke

kákke 'Ks', five symbols beginning with the letter 'k'

kaméez 'shirt'

kángha 'comb', one of the panj kakke

kára 'ring of steel', bangle, one of the panj kakke

karáh prashád sacred food received at a gurdwara

kaur 'prince', next in line to the crown prince, surname used by Sikh women and girls (sometimes translated as 'princess')

kes 'hair', one of the panj kakke

Khálsa 'pure ones', the community of Sikhs who have taken amrit

khánda 'broad-sword' with a double edge

kirpán 'sabre', sword, one of the panj kakke

kírtan the singing of religious songs

lángar 'public kitchen' and the food served from a langar

Lávan religious songs during the marriage ceremony

mánji sáhib wooden rectangular base on which the Guru Granth Sahib is placed

Mool Mantra basic statement of Sikh beliefs

nadar grace, goodness of the True Guru, God

nam 'name', the True Guru, God

nishán sáhib 'flag', 'banner', 'standard'

nit-nem 'daily rule', book of daily prayers from the Guru Granth Sahib and the Dasam Granth

pag 'turban'

págra 'large turban'

págri 'turban'

Panj Píare 'five loved ones' the first five people to take amrit from Guru Gobind Singh

panth 'path', 'way', 'road', beliefs and teachings, a community sharing the same religion

pátka 'small turban'

Rahirás prayers said in the evening

Rahít Maryada code of discipline and behaviour

rumál 'handkerchief' which can be worn to cover the head

rumála cloth which covers the Guru Granth Sahib

saháj path 'steady reading', non-continuous reading of the Guru Granth Sahib

sáhib 'lord', 'master', 'sir'

salwár 'trousers' worn by women

sángat 'company', congregation of people in a gurdwara

Sangránd first day of the month

sardar 'chief', form of address for a Sikh man

sat pathar 'seven stones', a team game from the Punjab

séva voluntary work, service or worship in the gurdwara or the community

shabad 'words', songs and prayers in the Guru Granth Sahib and the Dasam Granth

singh 'lion', surname used by Sikh men and boys

Sohíla prayer said before going to bed

Súkhmani Song of Peace, prayer said in the early morning

takht 'throne' and the raised platform supporting the manji sahib

Vahiguru/Waheguru 'Wonderful Guru', Wonderful Lord

Index

NB Words in the index refer to where the topic is discussed and not only to where the actual words occur.